★★★★★
MLB TEAMS

Detroit TIGERS

KENNY ABDO

Fly!
An Imprint of Abdo Zoom
abdobooks.com

abdobooks.com

Published by Abdo Zoom, a division of ABDO, P.O. Box 398166, Minneapolis, Minnesota 55439.

Printed in the United States of America, North Mankato, Minnesota.
102025
012026

THIS BOOK CONTAINS RECYCLED MATERIALS

Photo Credits: Alamy, AP Images, Getty Images, Shutterstock
Production Contributors: Kenny Abdo, Jennie Forsberg, Grace Hansen
Design Contributors: Candice Keimig, Neil Klinepier

Library of Congress Control Number: 2025936773

Publisher's Cataloging-in-Publication Data

Names: Abdo, Kenny, author.
Title: Detroit Tigers / by Kenny Abdo
Description: Minneapolis, Minnesota : Abdo Zoom, 2026 | Series: MLB teams | Includes online resources and index.
Identifiers: ISBN 9798384940180 (lib. bdg.) | ISBN 9798384940944 (ebook) | ISBN 9798384941323 (read-to-me ebook)
Subjects: LCSH: Detroit Tigers (Baseball team)--Juvenile literature. | Baseball teams--Juvenile literature. | Professional sports--Juvenile literature. | Sports franchises--Juvenile literature. | Major League Baseball (Organization)--Juvenile literature.
Classification: DDC 796.357--dc23

Table of CONTENTS

TIGERS

With bold energy and fierce spirit, the Tigers come into every game ready to roar. In Detroit, it would be a **catastrophe** for any rival to doubt them!

KALINE'

With a batting cage full of Hall of Famers, World Series wins, and **records**, the Tigers have an amazing history that unites fans across Motor City!

BATTER UP!

The Detroit Tigers were formed in 1894 and joined Major League Baseball (MLB) in 1901. The team's first game was against the Brewers the same year. Although they did not win, the Tigers bounced back quickly to make a name for themselves.

DETROIT

In 1907, the Tigers won their first **American League (AL) pennant**. The team kept the spark alive and reached the World Series three years in a row through 1909!

Even though they did not win any of the series, the Tigers got a taste of the championship and kept chasing it!

In 1935, the Tigers finally won their first World Series title! They defeated the Cubs in six games. This victory became a proud moment in Tigers history.

Detroit

GRAND SLAMS

The Tigers continued to shine, winning the World Series again in 1945! They defeated the Cubs once more. Fans across Detroit cheered proudly for their second championship.

In 1968, the Tigers had another season to remember. The team finished with 103 wins and took home the **AL pennant**. They went on to beat the St. Louis Cardinals in the World Series, bringing home a third title!

The Tigers had a strong run in the 1980s, with the 1984 season being the highlight. The team won the World Series that year by beating the San Diego Padres in five games. The Tigers finished the season with an amazing 104–58 **record**.

Tigers
CLINCHED
CLINCHED
CLINCHED
CLINCHED
OCTOBER READY

The Tigers made it to the World Series in 2006 and 2012. They lost to the Cardinals and San Francisco Giants, respectively. However, the Tigers still ruled the **AL** Central by winning four straight **division** titles from 2011 to 2014.

After a nine-year playoff **drought**, the Tigers made a strong comeback in 2024, winning the **Wild Card Series**. But they fell to the Guardians in a close **AL Division** Series (ALDS). The Tigers repeated their 2024 performance in the 2025 ALDS, losing to the Mariners in five games. Fans saw, however, that the Tigers were trending up.

HALL OF FAME

Ty Cobb is considered one of the best hitters in Tigers and MLB history. He had a .366 career batting average and 4,191 hits. Cobb set many **records** during his time, and some still stand today. He entered the Baseball Hall of Fame in 1936.

Al Kaline played his entire 22-year career with the Tigers. He won 10 **Gold Gloves** as a right fielder and became an 18-time **All-Star**. Kaline also won a batting title and helped the Tigers win a World Series. He remains one of the most beloved players in team history.

Lou Whitaker earned his stripes with the Tigers through many great moments on the field. He played a big role in the 1984 World Series win and earned five **All-Star** selections and three **Gold Gloves**. In 1989, he hit 28 home runs, the most by a Tigers second baseman in a single season. Ian Kinsler matched that in 2016.

WHITAKE

GLOSSARY

All-Star – an athlete named to the yearly baseball contest where top players from the AL and the National League (NL) compete against each other.

American League (AL) – one of two 15-team leagues that make up MLB.

catastrophe – utter failure.

division – a number of teams grouped together in a sport for competitive purposes.

drought – a long period of time when a team does not win a major title or playoff series.

Gold Glove Award – an annual award given to the best fielders at each position in both the AL and NL.

pennant – the title achieved by the team that wins its division or league championship.

record – a team's season total of wins and losses; a top achievement by a player or team that no one has done before.

Wild Card Series – the first round of the postseason.

ONLINE RESOURCES

Booklinks
NONFICTION NETWORK
FREE! ONLINE NONFICTION RESOURCES

To learn more about the Detroit Tigers, please visit **abdobooklinks.com** or scan this QR code. These links are routinely monitored and updated to provide the most current information available.

INDEX